I0105471

SPARKLE LIKE MARKLE

Laura Shenton

SPARKLE LIKE MARKLE

Laura Shenton

Iridescent Toad Publishing

Iridescent Toad Publishing.

© Laura Shenton 2023.
All rights reserved.

Laura Shenton asserts the moral right to be identified as the author of this work.

No part of this publication may be reproduced, stored or transmitted in any form or by any means, electronic, mechanical, photocopying, recording, scanning, or otherwise without written permission from the publisher. It is illegal to copy this book, post it to a website, or distribute it by any other means without permission.

Designations used by companies to distinguish their products are often claimed as trademarks. All brand names and product names used in this book and on its cover are trade names, service marks, trademarks and registered trademarks of their respective owners. The publishers and the book are not associated with any product or vendor mentioned in this book. None of the companies referenced within the book have endorsed the book.

All cover images used under a commercial license.

First edition. ISBN: 978-1-913779-90-0

"We want girls to grow up knowing their worth. When they have that sense of confidence, they excel in academics, in relationships, in extra curricular. Knowing their value dictates the choices they make."

- Meghan Markle
(as quoted in *Elle Magazine Canada*, October 2015).

Preface

I have never been a royalist. I don't dislike the royal family. I don't feel an intense extent of passion towards them, either. I see them as a British institution that, for better or worse, divides the opinion of many. For some, they are an integral part of our history, culture, and society; there to bring a boost in morale and to bring out the best in people. Indeed, in terms of relatively recent history, I'm sure that the TV speech the Queen delivered in April 2020, not long after the dire reality of the COVID-19 situation had hit the UK, served to at least touch a nerve for even the British people most impartial towards the royal family (even if it was just that poignant bit at the end when Vera Lynn's 'We'll Meet Again' was played). And of course, in 2022, the Queen's Platinum Jubilee was a brilliant reason – or coincidental opportunity, depending on where your bias sits – to have a bank holiday and, in some neighbourhoods, go out for a slice of cake and a chat with the neighbours.

There will always be people who think that the monarchy should be abolished. Their opinion doesn't offend or inspire me either way. Although that's a separate conversation that goes way beyond the scope of this book, I'm keen to tell you where I sit (albeit pretty much on the fence). To clarify, I really do not have a strong opinion on the royal family. I know that it means a lot to many. I know that it angers many. I know that many aren't particularly bothered either way. Such is the joy and fascination of living in the democracy that is the UK.

When I tell you that I'm not writing this book as someone with a passionate investment in the royal family, I hope that should serve to demonstrate that my reasons for doing so are coming from a different place.

It is currently December 2022, and, like anyone who doesn't live under a rock, it has been impossible to avoid all the talk in the media (both mainstream and social) about Prince Harry and Meghan Markle's Netflix documentary. As someone who enjoys watching all kinds of things on TV, I didn't feel a particular drive as to whether or not I wanted to watch the documentary either way. But curiosity got the better of me.

Based on the above, I hope it is clear that I began

watching the documentary with an open mind – my bias minimal, my passion unstirred as I scoffed my way through whatever midnight snack I had decided to indulge in.

Anyway, by episode two, I was crying. Having had no strong opinion towards Meghan either way up until that point, it suddenly dawned on me: here is a young woman who had built an amazing and exciting life for herself way before Harry had come into the picture.

I hadn't known much about Meghan prior to that. I just thought of her as "that American actress who married Prince Harry and has been given a fair bit of stick for it". In learning more about Meghan the individual, rather than Meghan, wife of Harry, I suddenly felt so saddened to learn of all the horrible things that she has been put through by the mainstream British media.

In writing this book, there are a number of things that I wish to communicate. Firstly, I want to put as much light as I possibly can on what Meghan achieved in her life prior to being involved with Harry. With the way that the British media sometimes talks about her, it would be easy to think that she hadn't achieved much, and hadn't really done anything of note. I see this book as an opportunity to offer insight into the successful

Meghan, the entrepreneurial, creative, and inspiring Meghan.

Secondly, I would also like to delve into the subject of Meghan Markle from a sociological perspective. There are all kinds of reasons as to why some of the British media, and indeed the British public, may hold some of the wildest extents of hurtful bias towards her. Not only do I want to address that, but to examine it too. Why? Because how can any society progress if it doesn't stop to ask questions? Questions such as, "Why is this person being so vilified?" and "From what stance are the perpetrators coming from in the first place? What's their initial bias? Where is this coming from?" and in relation to that, "Is it valid?" and if so, "To what extent?".

Largely under the umbrella of sociology, I will delve into the mechanics of how the media works. If we are to look at it as a machine, a construct even, then really, we have to examine the extent to which we can trust and value it. I mean, even this here book is a form of media. That said, there is a tremendous amount of difference between the process of writing a book, and writing for a newspaper.

Anyone who works in any form of journalism related to the sale of daily newspapers, for those guys, the pressure is *on*. They have a limited amount of time in which to get the material for their story, and then get it all written up into a narrative that the paper's editor is happy to run with. The industry overall is fast-moving, and it's vital to get dramatic, edgy, headlines and stories that are going to get those papers sold – every day! A lot of the same information will be printed in several papers due to how each of them wants to keep their readers engaged with current affairs. No publication wants to be left behind. Most want to be a leader in the field and so, for the big stories, there's a lot of money to be made. And that's all before taking into account the financial incentive for photographers to get exclusive photos. They can go for big money. All of these factors serve to build a picture of what can motivate a journalist whose job it is to create content for a daily newspaper. There is arguably a sense of urgency that fuels the way they react towards any subject that they may be desperate to get a big story on.

When it comes to writing a book, the process is, to a considerable extent, less intense. In my experience, it is about creating something that you want to last. The economics of it is that if your book isn't picked up by readers today, then maybe they'll read it another time. The timeline being worked to is far more generous than that which any media journalist would have the luxury of. Even taking the economics out of the equation, writing a book is different to newspaper journalism in the sense that you're not necessarily looking for a sensational story, or an exclusive. In writing a book, the scope is broader, and there's more opportunity to bring a unique narrative to the table. Sure, there will always be some form of bias present in every form of media out there, but when it comes to a book, unless the people making it are going for a particularly scandalous, tell-all angle, then the whole process is a lot more relaxed. There is certainly no running around after people in the public eye who would rather be left alone (and all of the potential drama it entails).

I promise that this book will be objective. Is it pro-Meghan Markle? Yes. Come on, of course it is! Let's get that vital bias right down and out there before we really start to delve. Still though, will that bias be presented in a way that is done without heroine worship, and in a way that leaves you, the reader, plenty of scope to come to your own conclusions? Absolutely! I have no intention, or desire, to preach to anyone. Remember, I wasn't really that interested in the whole Meghan Markle thing until I watched the Netflix documentary and thought, "Bloody hell! This woman does not deserve the lynching she is getting from much of the UK media!".

So, what qualifies me to write this book? The first thing I want to say in response to that is that really, I am just one of many people who has an opinion. In that regard, I entirely forgive you if you might be thinking, "Who on earth is Laura Shenton, and what gives her the right to write this book?". As a writer though, my background is in the genre of music non-fiction. That means that I get to research and analyse the narrative of what musicians in the field of rock and pop music were doing in their careers. It's mostly retrospective stuff from the seventies and eighties. The scope of my books in that subject area is a great way to examine the deeper context of what was going on for an artist overall. So yes, as a research nerd who enjoys gathering lots of details and exploring the narrative of them, providing an objective exploration on a subject of interest is something that comes naturally to me.

When it comes to certain topics in the public eye, I'm driven by the desire to investigate and understand the phenomenology. I feel that through an academic lens, I can offer a relevant and thought-provoking analysis into how Meghan Markle has become so unjustly vilified by many in the British media. I want to break down the mechanics of what has happened so far. Nobody deserves to be bullied, ever, and when it happens in response to a cruel narrative designed to sell newspapers, I feel that it's important to question such material. Give it the spotlight that it demands, and then go through it with a big neon pink highlighter to call out the bullshit.

I have no affiliation with anyone I am writing about in this book. I am entirely comfortable with that. I trust that it will allow for maximum objectivity. If you're looking for the words from those who have been there, you should definitely watch the Harry and Meghan documentary on Netflix. It has, after all, been designed to align with the message that they personally wish to communicate. As for me, just think of me as your friendly armchair commentator who is keen to bring an academic exploration to the table; that's where I very much hope that this book will shine.

Chapter One – But You Don't Even Know Her!

The words of this chapter title are very much what some critics may say in response to the fact that I am writing this book. And they're right. I don't know Meghan Markle – and rightly so! When it comes to any famous person, the only people who truly know them are those in their close circle. It's the same for any of us. Do our colleagues know the real us? Do the people who only see a combination of our social media profiles know us? No! And hey, that's normal.

There's actually a term that sums up the illusionary experience whereby someone may feel that they know a famous person simply through having only engaged with their work that's in the public eye: parasocial interaction. A term coined by sociologists Richard Wohl and Donald Horton in 1956, it's basically the idea that a false familiarity comes about, blurring the line between what we think we know, and what we actually know.

Following frequent engagement with media that features the person in the public eye, someone experiencing parasocial interaction reaches the point where they begin to think of that person as someone they actually know, perhaps even as a friend.

Whilst the majority of people who consume any media about someone in the public eye may not experience parasocial interaction to the extent that they begin to think of that person as a familiar, there is certainly an element of the concept at play when it comes to how any member of the public may begin to consume media about a famous person – especially in a media-heavy society where they are presented with an abundance of coverage on a particular subject.

When it comes to any famous person, their public persona may seem fun and friendly, but behind closed doors, they could be miserable and tedious to be around (or vice versa). We simply don't know, and vitally, it is due to a boundary of privacy that the famous person is absolutely entitled to, but more than that, it can fuel a sense of mystery. It's that same sense of mystery that can offer so much scope for anyone to put any kind of connotations that they want to onto the subject of interest: in this case, Meghan Markle.

So no, I don't know her. You don't know her. Most of the people who have ever written or said anything about her don't know her. And that's ok.

There's that popular concept about how in every point of argument in life, there's person A's version, person B's, person C's etc. – and then somewhere, in between a mixture of all of those, is the truth. Within all the nooks and crannies of what has been written about Meghan Markle in recent years, the truth has probably well and truly fallen through the cracks. We can't change that. What we can do, however, is examine what has happened as best as we can within what we do know (whilst remaining gracious about that which we don't know).

Like so many other people in the public eye, Meghan Markle has become a blank canvas onto which anyone can project their own choice of narrative or bias. What's particularly noteworthy though, is that overall, the narrative has generally shifted throughout various points in her time as a famous person.

From 2010 to 2016, the mainstream media was predominantly very flattering in their commentary on Meghan. Women's magazines would do the occasional feature on how glamorous she looked, and on how she was a nice, fun, down-to-earth person to interview over a relaxed coffee in Toronto. Newspapers with a more generalised audience would typically touch on the same, but comment more on how Markle was very much an actress with a stellar future ahead, having watched her play one of the lead characters in *Suits* (which was filmed in Toronto, hence why Meghan was often interviewed there by journalists who typically wrote well of her and spoke of how much they appreciated her – apparently humble – company).

Now, I haven't watched *Suits*. I have heard of it, and since having watched Harry and Meghan's Netflix documentary, I have seen clips of it – and that's how I'm going to keep it whilst writing this book. Again, I am not some hardcore fan of Meghan's who is rushing to speak in defence of her because I know and love everything that she's ever done. I, like many, have become interested in her on the basis of "How can the media be so cruel to somebody, who, really, hasn't particularly done anything to warrant such outcome?".

As has been mentioned in the Netflix documentary, the British media have been, on the whole, brutal in their systemic character assassination of Markle. Considering that Britain is a country that prides itself on its legal stance of "innocent until proven guilty", our media have done a rubbish job of embracing such approach when it comes to how they have really had the knives out for Meghan.

The British media's treatment of Markle has been, frankly, bizarre. They can literally take a photograph of her doing anything in the lexicon of a normal day-to-day life, and twist it into anything they like. For instance, if they were to get a photograph of something so mundane as Markle making a cup of tea, they could give it any narrative of their choosing. "Wife nearly scalds poor husband whilst making a brew", is an immensely different headline in comparison to "Wife lovingly makes a cuppa for her dear husband". Now then, as far as I'm aware, that example isn't something that has actually happened, and I would like to be able to say that it's too farfetched to be relatable. Sadly though, it's not too far removed from reality:

"Meghan made Kate cry." (from *The Sun* in November 2018).

"DEAR MEGHAN, we want to love you, but YOU'RE not making it easy with your 'poor me' attitude and royal paranoia." (from *The Sun* in July 2019).

"BRIDE & FUME. Meghan Markle 'embarrassed' Prince Harry by announcing pregnancy on Princess

Eugenie's wedding day, new book claims." (from *The Sun* in June 2020. They reported that "The Duchess of Sussex allegedly told the royal family that she was pregnant with the pair's first child at the nuptials in October 2018" and that "In their new book *Royals At War*, authors Andy Tillett and Dylan Howard claimed Eugenie and her mother Sarah Ferguson were 'furious' at Meghan's decision.").

"Meghan Markle 'ignored advice from Camilla on how to be a royal and handle bad media headlines before her marriage to Prince Harry'." (from *The Daily Mail* in August 2020).

"No going back: Meghan and Harry will NEVER be able to reverse Megxit pain – fans lash out." (from *The Daily Express* in December 2020).

"Prince Harry and Meghan Markle saga took 'terrible toll' on the Queen." (from *The Daily Express* in December 2022).

"Meghan Markle accused of 'projecting disdain' for UK and 'openly mocking' British people." (from *The Daily Express* in December 2022. They elaborated under the headline: "The documentary series on Netflix from Meghan Markle and Prince Harry has been met with an angry backlash from many viewers.").

It is headlines like the above that justify a need to write in defence of Meghan Markle – not because we know her, but because the sheer absurdity and level of negative speculation that she has been put under is not normal, and not healthy. As a society, if we don't question this, then what does that say about all of us? Do we want to participate in the scapegoating of a stranger, whose actions we aren't truly privy to, or do we want to stand up and question what we're being fed by the British media in particular? There is always junk food available, but do we really want to consume it without asking at least a few questions first?

Journalist Benjamin Ryan, a science reporter who has written for *The New York Times*, NBC News, and *The Guardian*, posted on his Twitter account in July 2022 that "Hating Meghan Markle is a billion dollar industry. It will never stop. Too many people make a living off it". There is certainly validity to this theory. As I mentioned earlier in the preface of this here book, there is a financial motivation at play when it comes to the journalists who report on Meghan Markle, or indeed, any other subject that gets the public's attention.

The subject of Markle in particular is one that can play on the public's emotions. It is entirely plausible that, based on the monster that the British media keep choosing to feed, there is a proportion of

British society who are chomping at the bit to know what awful things Markle has done recently, for, she has, after all, caused so much chaos according to much of the media's narrative. In terms of Meghan's interactions with the royals (or even the very fact that she exists), there are feelings amongst some of the public in the lexicon of anger and hatred. Ultimately, when the media move to further feed that narrative, this is stuff that *sells*. There *is* money to be made there.

So is the financial motive to push the hateful narrative on Meghan the only one that fuels the UK media's vitriol towards her? Well, truthfully, that is a question that nobody can answer. Nobody will ever be able to get an honest response from every single journalist who has ever participated in pushing the negative narrative on Markle. Perhaps it was a slow news day and they needed to come up with something quickly. Perhaps they wanted to create a spin that would give their article, and the paper it was to be printed in, a particular edge. Or hey, perhaps they really do have an absolute and genuine dislike of Markle, and are only too happy to have their thoughts on the matter brought to light in a public forum. Maybe they even feel that they are doing a worthwhile service to, as they may see it, those who wish to uphold the traditional values and aspirations of the royal family (whatever those might be, according to the opinion of any one individual that you may choose to ask).

Based on the range of variables that could be at play when it comes to the motives of anyone who chooses to write negatively about Meghan as part of their journalistic career, the fact is that we will never know what's at the heart of their reasons why. In a way, this is part of the problem, in the sense that, nobody will ever be able to agree on what's right, what's fair, what's appropriate, and what should be done in order to move forward (if anything!).

Anyone though, who is curious, or even frankly appalled, at the way in which Meghan has been portrayed by the UK media, has every right to pull that into question. There is no battle to be won here. As long as the media aren't breaking any laws in how they go about it, they can continue to say a great many awful things about anyone who happens to be a hot target at any given time. That's not something that can be stopped. What can be done, however, is an extent of analysis that will serve to bring a greater sense of balance to the table. Will it make a difference on a wider level, or will it provide food for thought to just a few individuals who have taken the time to engage with it? We don't know, but in the name of wanting to give any human being in the public eye a chance at a fair representation, or at least, consideration, we can certainly try.

Chapter Two – A Star in Her Own Right

There is no denying that throughout her career, Meghan Markle has done some wonderful, inspiring things. This was the case before her life with Harry, and it is still very much the case today. From a young age, she was engaged with the world around her, and had a passion for people, justice, the arts, and creative expression. The following is possibly only a snapshot of what Meghan has achieved so far, but it certainly serves to prove that she is undoubtedly a star in her own right.

Rachel Meghan Markle was born on 4th August 1981, at West Park Hospital in Canoga Park, Los Angeles, California. When she was two years old, her parents separated. Four years later, they got divorced. Meghan's father, Thomas Markle Sr. (born 1944), is an Emmy Award-winning TV lighting director and director of photography. He worked on the sets of *General Hospital* and

Married... With Children, which Meghan would occasionally visit. In more recent years, she has been estranged from her father and paternal half-siblings, Samantha Markle and Thomas Markle Jr.

Growing up in Los Angeles, Meghan attended Hollywood Little Red Schoolhouse. Both of her parents participated in her upbringing until she was nine years old, upon which, her father became the main caregiver, whilst her mother, Doria Ragland (born 1956), pursued a career. To this day, Meghan has maintained a close relationship with her mother.

When Meghan was eleven, along with her classmates, she wrote a letter to Proctor & Gamble, asking that they remove the gender stereotyping ("The gloves are coming off. Women are fighting greasy pots and pans with Ivory Clear.") from a national TV advertising campaign for their dish-washing product. Further to this, she appeared in an interview on children's network Nickelodeon, saying she was "furious" at the advert and that "it makes me think that they're going to grow up thinking that girls are less than them – you know, like boys are better than girls".

Although she wasn't raised as a Catholic, Meghan went to a Los Angeles all-girl Catholic school: Immaculate Heart High School. Whilst there, she participated in plays and musicals. Her father helped out with the lighting for them. Meghan worked at a local frozen yogurt shop during her teens, and then later as a waitress and babysitter. She also volunteered at a soup kitchen in Skid Row.

In 1999, she enrolled at Northwestern University in Evanston, Illinois. During her time there, she participated in a multitude of charity projects. In May 2018, *The Chicago Tribune* ran a feature titled "Meghan Markle recalled as dignified, charitable during her Northwestern days".

For the article, the paper got in touch with over 140 of Markle's Kappa Kappa Gamma sorority sisters, in hopes of being able to get more insight into what she was like during her time at Northwestern University. Although most of the women who were contacted didn't respond, those who did stated that Meghan "was always very kind", "is a delightful person", and "is a truly wonderful person". Another stated that even when sorority life could feel intimidating for newcomers, Meghan "was always very, very keen to make it as warm and welcoming as she could".

The paper quoted the response that was offered to them by Coulter Bump, who, by then working as a law attorney in Colorado, had been a member of

Kappa Kappa Gamma with Meghan: "We just wanted to be sure that we secured her interest in our sorority. Myself and most of my sisters agreed that she just is a really lovely person. She is respectful and polite. She always had this manner to her of being dignified and poised, just very appropriate in every circumstance. A person like that is what I wanted to ensure we had in our house and luckily, she liked us back."

Whilst with the sorority, Meghan volunteered with the Glass Slipper Project, an organisation that helps to match disadvantaged teens with donated outfits to wear for the prom – a vital coming of age occasion for any young American.

Following her junior year, with help from her uncle Michael Markle, Meghan secured an internship as a junior press officer at the American embassy in Buenos Aires. It was around this time that she was considering a career in politics. She also participated in a study abroad program, which saw her spend some time in Madrid.

In 2003, Meghan graduated from Northwestern's School of Communication with a bachelor's degree: a double major in theatre and international studies.

Meghan identifies as mixed race ("My dad is

Caucasian and my mom is African American. I'm half black and half white."). She has attributed this to some of the difficulties that she experienced at the beginning of her professional acting career, stating that she was "ethnically ambiguous": "I wasn't black enough for the black roles and I wasn't white enough for the white ones". To earn an income whilst between acting jobs, Meghan taught bookbinding and worked as a freelance calligrapher.

Her persistence paid off, and, with a little help from her personal connections, she managed to get a small TV acting role where she played a nurse in an episode of the daytime soap opera, *General Hospital*.

Small guest roles on TV soon followed. She appeared on *Century City* (2004), *The War At Home* (2006) and *CSI: NY* (2006). As well as several contract acting and modelling jobs, between 2006 and 2007, Meghan worked as a "briefcase girl" on *Deal Or No Deal* (US version). She appeared in the Fox series, *Fringe*, where she played Junior Agent Amy Jessup in the first two episodes of the show's second season.

In 2010, Markle featured in small roles in the films *Get Him To The Greek*, *Remember Me* (which was produced by her then-partner Trevor Engelson) and

The Candidate. The following year, she was in *Horrible Bosses*. She joined the cast of the USA Network show *Suits* in July 2011. She stayed with the show up until late 2017, by which time it was in its seventh season. She played the character of Rachel Zane, who began as a paralegal and eventually became an attorney. For each year of her time spent working on *Suits*, Meghan stayed in Toronto for nine months. In 2017, *Fortune* magazine estimated that she had been paid $50,000 per episode, equivalent to an annual salary of $450,000.

From 2010 to 2012, Meghan anonymously ran the blog, The Working Actress. It put the spotlight on the "pitfalls and triumphs of struggling to make it in Hollywood". In 2014, she founded The Tig. Her own lifestyle blog, it featured articles on fashion, beauty, travel, food, and inspirational women. Markle promoted the blog through her social media platforms, and was able to target around three million followers on Instagram, 800,000 on Facebook, and 350,000 on Twitter.

The Tig would go on to promote Meghan as a brand, and as a business woman, up until when she closed it in April 2017. In January 2018, she removed all of the articles from the website, as well as deleting all of her social media accounts.

Through The Tig, Meghan was able to promote her sense of fashion. She released two collections with Canadian clothing company Reitmans in 2015 and 2016. The lines were inspired by a blend of her personal style, and that of her *Suits* character.

In 2016, in collaboration with Lexus and Eater, Meghan hosted USA Network's video series, *Power Lunch With Meghan Markle*, in which she discussed the culinary inspirations of five different kitchens in New York.

In October 2017, Markle was featured on *Vanity Fair*'s cover story, and in December, in *Elle France*. Not long after the announcement of her engagement to Prince Harry in the November, when she took one of the brand's handbags to a public event, there was a surge of public interest in Scottish retailer, Strathberry. As *The Telegraph* reported in December 2017, "Scottish family handbag firm feels the 'Meghan effect' as Strathberry orders soar". It was anticipated that, just as had been the case with Kate Middleton, Meghan's fashion sense would result in sales for the brands she wore.

Indeed, following Meghan and Harry's earlier appearances as a couple, a number of brands saw an increase in their website hits and sales. This included Birks, Mackage, Crown Jewellers, R&R Jewellers, and Everlane. In May 2018, *British*

Vogue speculated that Meghan's fashion influence would create broad waves on an international basis due to her fanbase in America. In the US, sales of yellow gold jewellery increased in the first quarter of 2018.

Following the announcement of her pregnancy, Meghan appeared in a Karen Gee dress. It resulted in the Australian designer's website crashing. As *Harper's Bazaar* put it on 16th October 2018, "Designer Karen Gee's website crashed after the Duchess of Sussex wowed onlookers in a simple ivory shift as she greeted government officials with Prince Harry on day one of their Australian tour. Despite the pregnancy announcement Monday by Kensington Palace, the dress showed a barely visible baby bump."

Meghan was nominated for the 2018 Teen Choice Awards in the Choice Style Icon category. Also that year, along with other senior royal women, *Tatler* included her in its list of Britain's best-dressed people.

In 2019, British brand Reiss reported an increase in sales after Meghan was seen on International Women's Day wearing one of their dresses. In 2022, the Fashion Museum Bath selected the black Armani dress worn by Meghan during her Oprah interview as dress of the year 2021.

In 2018, *Time* magazine listed Meghan as one of the 100 most influential people in the world. The publication also placed her on its shortlist for person of the year. In 2021, her name appeared on the list again, and she was featured with Harry on one of the magazine's seven worldwide covers. In 2019, the magazine named Meghan and Harry among the twenty-five most influential people on the internet. In 2018, 2019, and 2021, *British Vogue* listed Meghan as one of the twenty-five most influential women in the UK.

In June 2021, *The Bench*, a picture book written by Meghan, was published by Random House Children's Books. Following the book's release, Meghan donated 2,000 copies of it to libraries, schools, and other non-profit organisations across the US. On 17th June, the book got to number one on *The New York Times* best sellers list in the children's picture book category.

Based on her perception of the relationship between her husband and their son, the book was met with a mixed response. Whilst it was praised for its illustrations and overall message, it was criticised for its writing and structure. It was "lacking a good story and basic rhythm" and "rather than entertainment for children, this reads as a self-help manual for needy parents," said Alex O'Connell, reviewing it for *The Times*. The *Evening Standard* described it as "soothing, loving, although a little schmaltzy in places".

In July 2021, it was announced that in partnership with David Furnish, Meghan would executive-produce a Netflix animated series. Titled *Pearl*, the series had originally been pitched to Netflix in 2018. Planned as a depiction of the adventures of a twelve-year-old girl inspired by influential women from history, the project was cancelled in May 2022.

In 2022, Meghan was listed by *Worth* magazine as one of the fifty women changing the world over the past year. Also, *Variety* named her as a stellar honouree for its power of women issue. The *Financial Times* included her on its list of the twenty-five most influential women of 2022.

Meghan has achieved a range of things that, as single accomplishments, would be the icing on the cake for many people. Not only that, but evidently, there are still plenty of media publications that have many positive things to say about her – both in their reporting of what she has done, and in terms of their narrative thereof. It is reassuring to acknowledge that not *everyone* in the media wishes to paint Meghan Markle in a bad light, it's just that the ones who do, are, sadly, unforgettable...

Chapter Three – You Can Count on The Daily Mail…

To be clear, the issue of how the British media has been towards Meghan Markle does not just rest at the door of any one particular publication. If that was the case, then it would probably have been easier for the British public, and for Meghan herself, to simply shrug it off that one paper was pushing an overzealous extent of bias whilst the others were gracefully taking a more balanced approach.

Sadly, the reality is that whilst *The Daily Mail* was one of the first British newspapers to run such a memorably brutal story on Markle, most of the others have done so too. For what it's worth, in a 2017 survey carried out by The European Broadcasting Union, participants voted that, in their opinion, UK newspapers were the least trustworthy out of all twenty-eight EU countries in question.

What stands out in particular about *The Daily Mail*, however, is that around the time that the British media had really started to write unfavourably of Markle, the publication ran a story that, in the opinion of many, held racist connotations.

Meghan began her relationship with Prince Harry in mid-2016. The couple claim to have first connected with each other through Instagram, having been put in touch via a mutual friend. On the 8th November of that year, Harry found himself having to direct his communications secretary to release a statement on his behalf, expressing personal concern about the pejorative and false comments made about Meghan by mainstream media and internet trolls. Following this, in a letter to a British media regulator, Markle's representatives complained of harassment from journalists.

The statement directed by Harry, deplored the "racist" and "sexist" commentary and coverage of Meghan, expressing that "the past week has seen a line crossed". It described her as having been "subject to a wave of abuse and harassment. Some of this has been very public – the smear on the front page of a national newspaper; the racial undertones of comment pieces; and the outright sexism and racism of social media trolls and web article comments". The statement asserted that this had given Harry cause for concern about Meghan's safety. It concluded that Harry's purpose in issuing it was "in the hopes that those in the press who have been driving this story can pause and reflect before any further damage is done".

The couple's concerns were not unfounded. On 2nd November 2016, *The Daily Mail* had published the headline, "Harry's girl is (almost) straight outta Compton: Gang-scarred home of her mother revealed – so will he be dropping by for tea?". The article, written by Ruth Styles, has been heavily criticised as being a prime example of the racist press commentary directed towards Meghan.

The article abundantly put a negative spin on Meghan's family background, honing in on her upbringing in the Los Angeles district of Crenshaw, and putting emphasis on the area's high crime rate ("Crenshaw has endured forty-seven crimes in the past week – including murder.").

The headline references the 1988 debut record by American gangsta rap hip-hop group N.W.A.: 'Straight Outta Compton'. The city in southern Los Angeles was historically notorious for gang violence. Notably though, Compton is fourteen miles from Crenshaw. Crenshaw suffered significant damage from both the 1992 Los Angeles riots and the 1994 Northridge earthquake, but in the late 2000s, through the help of redevelopment and gentrification, improved.

The first paragraph of the article stated; "Plagued by crime and riddled with street gangs, the troubled Los Angeles neighbourhood that Doria Ragland, sixty, calls home couldn't be more different to London's leafy Kensington. But social worker Ragland might now find herself welcoming a royal guest to downtrodden Crenshaw after Prince Harry was revealed to be dating her daughter – *Suits* actress Meghan Markle."

Vitally, *The Daily Mail* wasn't the only publication to run with a derogatory narrative centred on Meghan's background. On 3rd November, *The Daily Star*'s headline was "Harry to marry into gangster royalty? New love 'from crime-ridden neighbourhood'." Following this, the article stated, "Harry's hottie Meghan Markle comes from one of the city's roughest suburbs, famed for its gangland wars. And the royal's possible future mother-in-law still lives in Crenshaw, surrounded by bloodbath robberies and drug-induced violence. With ancestors freed from slavery, the American sweetheart's upbringing could form the perfect rags-to-riches story."

The trouble with the latter rhetoric surrounding Meghan is that it insinuates that she comes from a life of crime. From when she first came into the spotlight as Harry's girlfriend, it set a negative tone for how some of the UK media would continue to portray her, playing on harmful stereotypes.

Fortunately, not everyone in the media has been willing to sit on the fence and simply accept that the implied connotations projected onto Meghan have been acceptable. Writing for *The Guardian* in March 2021, activist and lawyer Shola Mos-Shogbamimu said that she could not "believe that we are still having this debate about whether the way that Meghan has been treated is racist. It is misogynoir, pure and simple. Look at the media coverage of her. *The Daily Mail* said that she was '(almost) straight outta Compton'... That tells you what kind of society we live in".

Notably, not all of the negative narrative directed towards Meghan in late 2016 was centred on her background; some of it was simply scandal for scandal's sake – and very much a cheap shot at trying to sell papers! In addition to *The Daily Mail*'s and *The Daily Star*'s derogatory spin on Markle in November 2016, *The Sun* ran the headline, "Harry's girl on Pornhub". The publication later denied any smear once it was revealed that, actually, the clips were simply scenes from *Suits*, and that the non-pornographic material had been illegally uploaded online. In February

2017, *The Sun* apologised for their actions in an official statement.

Throughout their Netflix documentary series, Meghan and Harry staunchly maintain that the media had been "destroying" them whilst they were in the UK. They highlighted a number of the headlines that held racist or misogynistic connotations, including "(almost) straight outta Compton". Then, in December 2022, in response to the documentary's release, Jeremy Clarkson wrote a column for *The Sun*, complaining that he hated Meghan "on a cellular level" and dreamed "of the day when she is made to parade naked through the streets of every town in Britain while the crowds chant, 'Shame!' and throw lumps of excrement at her".

More than 20,800 complaints were submitted to the Independent Press Standards Organisation in response to Clarkson's column. On 20th December 2022, Conservative MP Caroline Nokes wrote to *The Sun*'s editor, Victoria Newton, demanding that action be taken against Clarkson, and for an "undeserved apology". More than sixty cross-party MPs signed the letter. On 23rd December, *The Sun* issued an apology, stating that "columnists' opinions are their own" but they "regret the publication of this article" and are "sincerely sorry".

In response to the complaints that his article was in incredibly poor taste, Clarkson claimed that his comments about Meghan being made to walk naked in public were made in reference to a scene from *Game Of Thrones*. His vitriol does indeed have echoes of a famous scene from the show. In him saying that he got his detailed description of brutality from a well-known and popular TV drama series though, it seems to be an attempt – albeit feeble – to distance himself from having created such a foul scenario in his own mind. There's almost a sense that he's trying to say something along the lines of "it's based on a scene from something that exists in popular culture. It's not an alien concept and it's one that you were all aware of – you all saw it too!". Now, far be it from me to try and understand what goes on in Clarkson's head. However, the bottom line is that no matter how much he might try to justify his comments, the fact is that he went that low in the first place, and the damage has now been done.

Ironically perhaps, it could be argued that Clarkson's awful comments have served to prove the very point that Meghan and Harry have so graciously been trying to make for a while now, and have honed in on in their Netflix documentary: that a proportion of the British media are being below the belt in their commentary on Meghan in particular. Sure, it's not the first time that Jeremy

Clarkson has come under fire for having taken things too far in how he has gone about expressing his opinions. And of course, he is one of many famous journalists, many of whom wouldn't ever dare to go that far and risk the fallout and potentially career-damaging backlash. It could be argued that Clarkson is the exception, rather than the rule. Is that a likelihood though, considering that Meghan and Harry had voiced similar concerns about the British media even prior to the Clarkson scandal?

Chapter Four – Her Own Voice

By convention, members of the British royal family are supposed to present as being politically neutral. As someone who married into that, however, Meghan had already been politically active in her time prior. This presents a complex situation – not only in the sense that Meghan had already had a chance to express her political opinions in public, but in terms of how, going forward, anyone asking her to then censor the things that mean a lot to her was always going to be asking for something monumental.

Anyone marrying into royalty would have been up against the same expectations. Meghan though, in particular, has always been so politically engaged throughout her life, that even to ask her to simply tone down that part of herself was probably, never going to be realistic.

Meghan knows who she is, and knows what she stands for and against. She is, by all accounts, a person with conviction, and not somebody with a tendency to sit on the fence – especially when it comes to social justice. Whilst in most people, this is considered to be a potentially attractive quality, for Meghan in her capacity as a royal, it makes her something of an anomaly in terms of how explicitly she has flouted tradition, and vitally, *expectation.*

Now then, whether the latter is offensive or refreshing to any one individual out there, will very much depend on how they feel about what a royal family member should – and shouldn't – express in public. Meghan's political engagement has been a source of discomfort for many, but still, it is demonstrative of who she is, and what she cares about as an individual. She is not a neutral figurehead, and probably, never will be.

Following Meghan's marriage to Prince Harry in May 2018, just two months later, Irish Senator Catherine Noone tweeted that the Duchess was "pleased to see the result" of the Irish referendum on legalising abortion. As a result of this, Meghan received criticism for potentially having breached the protocol that prohibits royals from interfering in politics. In response to this, Noone deleted her tweet, emphasising that her statement was misleading and that "the Duchess was not in any way political".

Looking at Meghan's charitable and political engagements though, it would pretty much be impossible for anyone to sweep that aspect of who she is under the carpet. Conversely, it could be argued that there's a fine line between politics and charity. And indeed, other members of the royal family have often contributed to – and engaged with – charitable causes. In many ways, much of the charity work that Meghan has done in her capacity as a royal has been alongside other royals, and often for causes just as worthy as those which she has chosen to help under her own initiative. It's strange, in a way, that everyone in the royal family has been encouraged and supported when engaging with *approved* causes, whilst Meghan, by all accounts, would seem to be more outside of the norm in her overt engagement with *other* issues that still affect human beings, but just happen to be more *explicitly* political (for instance, the debate surrounding abortion).

In 2014, Meghan toured Spain, Italy, Turkey, Afghanistan and England with the United Service Organisations. Whilst in Toronto, she volunteered for the Community Meals Program of St Felix Centre, where she donated food from the set of *Suits*. Also in 2014, she was a counsellor for the international network, One Young World. She spoke at its summit in Dublin, and, in 2016, attended the opening ceremony in Ottawa.

For International Day of the Girl in October 2015, she led a day of workshops for youth and educators in Toronto, as part of the Dove Self-Esteem Project (since 2004, the project has provided education and workshops dedicated to helping the self-esteem of young people. It focuses on issues such as body confidence and bullying).

In 2016, Markle became a global ambassador for World Vision Canada, travelling to Rwanda for the Clean Water Campaign. Following a trip to India with a focus on raising awareness of women's issues, she wrote an op-ed for *Time* magazine, explaining the stigmatisation of women with regards to menstrual health. She has also worked with the United Nations Entity for Gender Equality and as an advocate for Empowerment of Women.

During the 2016 US president election, Meghan backed Hillary Clinton, and publically denounced Donald Trump. Also that year, when the UK voted in favour of terminating its membership of the European Union, Markle posted on Instagram to express her disappointment with the result. In 2017, she used the same platform to recommend the book, *Who Rules The World?* by left-wing intellectual Noam Chomsky.

Also in 2017, she and Harry teamed up with the charity, Elephants Without Borders, which saw them assisting with the conservation efforts in Botswana. It was announced in March 2020 that Markle would narrate Disneynature's documentary, *Elephant*, which was released on 3rd April. As part of the project, Disneynature and the Disney Conservation Fund pledged to donate to Elephants Without Borders.

In January 2018, Markle got involved with the Hubb Community Kitchen, managed by survivors of the Grenfell Tower fire. She visited often. Whilst there, she suggested that the displaced women publish a cookbook to assist in raising funds for the group. *Together: Our Community Cookbook*, announced in the September, was Meghan's first charity project as Duchess of Sussex. Notably, not only has Meghan continued to be vocal as a feminist, but has used her role as a member of the royal family to continue supporting women's rights and social justice.

In August 2020, Meghan used proceeds from the cookbook to donate £8,000 to Migrateful. The UK charity supports refugees, asylum seekers, and migrants. In March 2021, she donated £10,000 from the book's proceeds to Himmah. Also a UK-based charity, the money went towards stocking the group's food bank, providing them with equipment, and helping the Salaam Shalom Kitchen – the only Muslim and Jewish community kitchen in the UK.

In 2019, Meghan was a contributor and guest editor for the September issue of *British Vogue*. Through this, she highlighted the works of fifteen women from different areas, who were described as "forces for change". Editor-in-chief of the publication, Edward Enninful, later revealed that the issue had become the "fastest-selling issue in the history of *British Vogue*". Also included in the iconic issue, was coverage of Meghan's collaboration with several British fashion houses and stores to launch a capsule collection for September 2019. Called The Smart Set, the collection was for the benefit of the Smart Works charity. Its purpose was to help "unemployed and disadvantaged women", through selling items "on a one-for-one basis, meaning an item is donated for each item purchased". In just ten days, the collection managed to provide a year's worth of clothes for the charity.

In April 2020, amidst the early days of the COVID-19 pandemic in the US, Meghan and Harry volunteered to personally deliver foods prepared by Project Angel Food to residents in Los Angeles. In June, the couple backed the Stop Hate For Profit campaign, in which they encouraged CEOs from a number of companies to get involved. In July, Meghan spoke in support of the Black Lives Matter movement. In August, she and Harry collaborated with Baby2Baby, participating in drive-through distribution of school supplies.

Whilst in the US, and as an eligible voter, Meghan released a video with her husband, in which they encouraged others to register for the 2020 presidential election on National Voter Registration Day. Some of the media reported that the video was an explicit endorsement of Democratic candidate, Joe Biden.

In April 2021, Meghan and Harry were announced as campaign chairs for Vax Live: The Concert to Reunite the World. Organised by Global Citizen, the event's purpose was to increase access to COVID-19 vaccinations. The couple also announced their support for a vaccine equity fundraiser initiated by the same organisation, as well as writing an open letter to pharmaceutical industry CEOs, urging them to take action in response to the vaccine equity crisis.

To mark her fortieth birthday in August 2021, Meghan launched 40x40, a campaign that asks people around the world to volunteer forty minutes of their time mentoring women who wish to re-enter the workforce. In September, she and Harry spoke again in support of vaccine equity at the Global Citizen Live concert. The following month, and prior to the 2021 G20 Rome summit, along with Director-General of the World Health Organisation, Tedros Adhanom, they wrote an open letter, requesting that the G20 leaders increase engagement with efforts for the global distribution of COVID-19 vaccines.

In October 2021, Meghan wrote an open letter to Senate Majority Leader, Chuck Schumer, and House Speaker, Nancy Pelosi, advocating for paid leave for parents (she posted it on the website, PaidLeaveforAll.org). In the letter, she expressed herself not as an authority figure, but as a mother: "I'm not an elected official, and I'm not a politician. I am, like many, an engaged citizen and a parent. And because you and your congressional colleagues have a role in shaping family outcomes for generations to come, that's why I'm writing to you at this deeply important time – as a mom – to advocate for paid leave."

Meghan's comments were contested by Republican representatives Jason Smith and Lisa McClain, who found her statement "out of touch", and argued that, as someone with a British royal title, her interference with American politics was unacceptable.

According to ABC News in November 2021, Meghan lobbied senators from both parties on the issue of paid family leave, including Democratic senators Patty Murray and Kirsten Gillibrand, and Republican senators Shelley Moore Capito and Susan Collins.

In February 2022, Meghan was vocal in her support for the Supreme Court nomination of Ketanji Brown Jackson. She asserted that "Judge Jackson's nomination has opened new ground for women's representation at the highest level of a judicial system that for too long has tilted against the very community she hails from".

The same month, Meghan and Harry were selected to receive the President's Award from the National Association for the Advancement of Coloured People (NAACP) for their work on causes relating to social justice and equity. *Deadline* reported that in Meghan and Harry's speech, Meghan "highlighted the important work established by past civil rights leaders and urged the passage of voter protection laws to honour their legacies".

In March 2022, Meghan and Harry were among more than a hundred people who signed an open letter. Published by the People's Vaccine Alliance, it demanded free global access to COVID-19 vaccines, calling out the UK, the EU and Switzerland for opposing a waiver that would allow vaccine intellectual property protections to be lifted.

In June 2022, Meghan publically supported Moms Demand Action, an organisation campaigning for safer gun laws in the US. In the same month, in an interview with Jessica Yellin for *Vogue*, she criticised the US Supreme Court for their decision that abortion is not a protected constitutional right. Meghan has voiced her support for the proposed Equal Rights Amendment, and also voted in the 2022 US elections.

For their work on mental health, racial justice, and several other social initiatives through their foundation Archewell, Meghan and Harry were named as Ripple of Hope Award laureates in October 2022.

From January 2019 to February 2021, Meghan was patron of London's National Theatre and the Association of Commonwealth Universities. She continued her role as the private patron of Mayhew until 2022. Presently, she is still a private patron of Smart Works. Between March 2019 and February 2021, she was the vice president of The Queen's Commonwealth Trust. Up until February 2021, occasional online QCT chat sessions were conducted and uploaded to YouTube. Along with other members of the royal family, in October 2019, Meghan voiced a Public Health England announcement as part of the Every Mind Matters mental health program.

In February 2018, Meghan and Harry attended the first annual forum of The Royal Foundation. Following her marriage to Harry, Meghan became the foundation's fourth patron (alongside Prince Harry, Prince William and his wife, Kate). In May 2019, as part of their Heads Together initiative, they launched Shout, a text messaging service for people struggling with mental health issues. It was announced in June 2019 that Harry and Meghan would step away from the charity and establish their own foundation. Regardless though, Meghan and Harry, and William and Kate, have continued to work together on mutual projects.

In April 2020, Meghan and Harry set up their own foundation, Archewell. The name was registered in the US, and its website was launched officially in October 2020. They had previously set up a foundation under their Duke and Duchess of Sussex titles, but upon stepping away from their roles as official royals, they dissolved it prior to starting Archewell.

Chapter Five – The Oprah Interview

On 8th January 2020, Harry and Meghan announced on Instagram that they would "step back as 'senior' members" of the British royal family, dividing their time between the UK and North America, and being financially independent. The scenario was dubbed as 'Megxit' – a play on the term Brexit, and a portmanteau of the words 'Meghan' and 'exit'. The term 'Megxit' was adopted globally by mainstream and social media, resulting in a range of internet memes, and even Megxit merchandising (on 15th January, regarding the production and sales of clothing and souvenirs, *The Times* reported, "Megxit turns into a moneyspinner.").

The Sun is credited as having been the first to run a headline featuring the word 'Megxit' (on 9th January 2020). BBC News commented that 'Sussexit' was trending on social media, but it didn't take off in the mainstream media in the way that 'Megxit' did. Social data analytics firm Brandwatch insisted that actually, the term 'Megxit' had been in use on Twitter since at least early 2019 as part of several negative comments written about Meghan. Sky News also asserted that the term had been in circulation online since as far back as April 2019. Collins English Dictionary added 'Megxit' to its online edition as a top ten word of 2020. Collins told *The Times*: "It immediately caught on due to its echoes of 'Brexit'."

Meghan and Harry's announcement led to a meeting of the royal family on 13th January. Dubbed the "Sandringham Summit" by *The Daily Telegraph*, it resulted in the Queen issuing a rare personal statement on her family. Across both UK and US media outlets, she was praised for her rapid handling of the matter. On 18th January, an agreement was announced whereby Meghan and Harry would "no longer be working members of Britain's royal family", and would discontinue the use of their 'Royal Highness' styles.

The Sunday Mirror announced the outcome as a "hard Megxit" (*The Times* had previously speculated under the headline, "Hard or soft Megxit? What's on the table."). Writing for *The Sunday Times*, Camilla Long offered a particularly scathing commentary: "We've had the stupidity to pay this pair of oxygen thieves more than £60,000 a day, if you take into account the £32m wedding, the £2.4m cottage renovation, the security and fripperies and Meghan's dresses, for the privilege of being patronised and dissed to our faces by them, since they married in May 2018."

Writing for *The Mail on Sunday*, Hugo Vickers considered that by surrendering his royal status, Prince Harry could "lose his allure and appeal – and people could tire of them both". Interestingly, this particular narrative is a prime example of the way in which Harry's association with Meghan has been used against him: it's part of a wider idea that without Meghan in the picture, Harry wouldn't be running the risk of such alienation – both from his family, and in terms of public opinion. It could be argued that the use of Meghan's name – rather than Harry's – in the term 'Megxit', only serves to add emphasis to the idea that Meghan is to blame.

The couple was given a twelve-month review period, to allow for if they wanted to change their minds. Thereafter, on 19th February 2021, Buckingham Palace confirmed that Harry and Meghan would relinquish their royal patronages, and would not be returning as working members of the royal family. The announcement solidified the couple's decision to be independent of the royal family and its protocol.

In November 2021, as part of a *Wired* panel on combating internet misinformation, Harry said that "the term 'Megxit' was, or is, a misogynistic term, and it was created by a troll, amplified by royal correspondents, and it grew and grew and grew into mainstream media. But it began with a troll".

On 19th January 2020, *The Guardian* – a publication that has certainly been kinder in their representation of Meghan and Harry overall – assessed the reasoning behind the couple's decision, stating that Harry "lay the blame at the feet of the press". They also reported on how, at a private dinner in London for his charity Sentebale, Harry announced, "I know that you've come to know me well enough over all these years to trust that the woman I chose as my wife upholds the same values as I do. And she does". Also: "The decision that I have made for my wife and I to step back is not one I made lightly... there really was no other option."

The Guardian's assessment of the situation carried much weight, as would come to light when Meghan and Harry took the bold step to take the narrative surrounding their choice into their own hands.

In their TV interview with Oprah Winfrey in March 2021, Harry and Meghan explained that Megxit was due to them not getting the help they sought from the royal establishment – particularly in terms of how false tabloid stories about Meghan had not been refuted, and in how she was declined support for her mental health. In the interview, Harry also indicated that members of his family closest to the royal institution are trapped (he is not alone in his opinion. British constitutional scholar Robert Hazell argues that the institution requires some of its members to give up a significant extent of their human rights).

Filmed in Santa Barbara County, California, the interview came out just over a year after Harry and Meghan's announcement that they would be stepping down as working members of the royal family. In the US, the TV special premiered on CBS on 7th March 2021. In the UK, it was broadcast on ITV the next day.

The interview received high viewing figures, and was given extensive attention from the world's media. It was nominated for a 2021 Television Critics Award, a Primetime Emmy Award, and a People's Choice Award.

Although Meghan and Harry were not paid for the interview, other stakeholders benefitted from it substantially. The *Wall Street Journal* reported that CBS paid "a license fee of between $7m and $9m" for the broadcasting rights.

Prior to the interview, Meghan and Harry already had an established rapport with Oprah; she was a guest at their wedding. She was not the first to score an interview with them though. The couple had already been interviewed in the 2019 ITV documentary, *Harry and Meghan: An African Journey with Tom Bradby*. On 26th February 2021, a seventeen-minute feature that the couple had made with James Corden – including an interview with Harry on an open-top bus and a sketch starring all three of them – was broadcast as part of *The Late Late Show*. A friend of the couple, Corden told *Deadline*, "We're really proud of it, it was the first thing that Harry had done since stepping down or stepping away from the royal family. I've known him a very long time, and so we wanted to show the person that I know, the person I've known for a long time, and we just wanted it to be judged on what it was and what it is without a sort of massive speculation leading up to it such as the nature of the way that people talk about him and Meghan."

In their interview with Oprah, the couple discussed their courtship and their wedding. They also talked about a royal title for Archie, their personal security, and Harry's difficult relationships with his father, Charles, and brother, William. Meghan's relationship with her own estranged family was also mentioned.

In particular, the couple shed light on Meghan's suicidal thoughts, explaining that they felt a sense of abandonment in terms of a lack of emotional support from the institution. Further to this, Meghan stated that one or more comments had been made privately to Harry – by an unnamed individual within the royal family – regarding the skin colour of their then-unborn son, Archie Mountbatten-Windsor.

Meghan said in the interview, "I did not want to be alive anymore", elaborating that she had gone to several senior palace officials for help, or to be checked into a hospital, but was told that it would not be possible due to the bad publicity it could generate.

On the human rights front, Meghan discussed feeling trapped, explaining that her driver's licence, passport, and credit cards had been taken from her prior to her wedding, and been made unavailable to her.

When Harry discussed Meghan's treatment, he drew comparisons to his late mother, stating that he was fearful for Meghan's safety ("I saw history repeating itself"). He explained that he stepped back from his royal position as a last resort once it had become clear that the help he was asking for would not be granted. He also asserted that following his and Meghan's tour of Australia in October 2018, some members of the royal family were jealous of "how good she [Meghan] was at the job", and of the "effortless" manner in which she had managed to establish a rapport with people in the Commonwealth.

The following day on *CBS This Morning*, four clips that hadn't been aired as part of the main programme were shown. In them, the couple discussed Meghan's tabloid coverage. Harry explained that, in his opinion, his ancestral family had adapted to a culture of "control and the fear by the UK tabloids". He also told Oprah that the UK tabloid press was "bigoted" and creates a "toxic environment".

Meghan added that her experience of joining the royal family was different to what sister-in-law Kate's had been, asserting that social media was different when Kate was going through a similar period of transition. Meghan also acknowledged that whilst the whole royal family has had to deal with bad press coverage over the years, only hers has been slanted with an element of racism.

Although not on good terms with him at the time,

she expressed sympathy for her father in how he was "hunted" by the press. She also spoke highly of her mother for her handling of the same situation "in silent dignity". Meghan added that she barely knew her half-sister Samantha Markle, and questioned the credibility of her decision to write a tell-all book.

O, The Oprah Magazine, released an additional clip from the interview. In it, Meghan talked about "a basic right to privacy". She acknowledged that, as public figures, she and her husband had never asked for complete privacy, but argued that it should be up to them to decide which aspects of their lives are put under the spotlight.

Speaking to the BBC, Katie Nicholl – author, journalist and royal commentator – argued that "Meghan isn't followed or chased by the paparazzi in the way Diana was", adding, "I think Meghan has come under just as much scrutiny as any other member of the Royal family".

Writing for *The Independent*, Rachel Brodsky considered that whilst the "couple may never be free from the tabloids' monster grip", their interview with Oprah was demonstrative of how in "taking back their narrative, they can be part of the conversation" and "that is their choice to make".

Writing for *The Daily Telegraph*, Anita Singh considered the interview as "a mix of straight-from-the-heart and stagey", asserting that it "was really the Meghan and Oprah show, and the two women complemented each other perfectly". Writing for the same publication, historian Andrew Roberts was adamant in his assessment, stating that the couple "took the deliberate decision to damage the institution of the monarchy as much as they possibly could on the way out". He added, "If the monarchy really is a sinister racist institution, Harry and Meghan ought to resign their HRH titles and the Duchy of Sussex forthwith".

Also writing for *The Daily Telegraph*, Allison Pearson was critical of the interview and the couple's attitude: "The only truthful lens is their own. Anyone who comes up with facts which contradict their feelings is either frightened of the tabloids, trapped or racist – quite possibly all three". She also argued that due to a lack of knowledge on the UK and the royal family, Winfrey wasn't qualified to carry out a balanced interview on the subject.

The Washington Post reported that the British media was reacting "in horror" to the interview. Unsurprisingly perhaps, the British tabloids, who were so heavily criticised in the interview, were particularly negative about the whole thing. *The*

Daily Mail ran the headline, "Toxic accusations, incendiary racism claims against their family. Palace left reeling and Queen, ninety-four, in emergency talks. After *that* stinging interview. What *have* they done?". "Palace in crisis", the front page of *The Guardian* stated, describing the couple's racism claim as "devastating". *The Telegraph* described Meghan and Harry's revelations as an "insult to the Queen". *The Daily Express* announced concern for how the interview would have an impact on the Queen, asserting "[it's] so sad it has come to this".

Following the Oprah interview, the US media was generally more sympathetic towards Meghan and Harry. "Throughout Meghan's time as a royal, the British tabloids have been particularly vicious and often racist in their coverage of her," *The Cut* advocated. *The Hollywood Reporter* argued, "*The Daily Mail* and its sister publication, *The Mail on Sunday*, have been particularly virulent in their coverage of the Sussexes". Notably, some of the more conservative media outlets in the US reacted negatively to the interview, placing emphasis on how it was damaging to the British monarchy.

Following the broadcast of the interview, on *Good Morning Britain*, Piers Morgan made comments about Meghan that attracted a record number of complaints to TV regulator Ofcom. Some 57,000 were made against Morgan's rant, in which he stated that he "didn't believe" a word Meghan had said, adding "the fact that she's fired up this onslaught against our royal family, I think is contemptible".

In his commentary, Morgan picked up on Meghan's revelation that, following suicidal thoughts, her request to senior Buckingham Palace officials for help was rejected. "Who did you go to?" he said. "What did they say to you? I'm sorry, I don't believe a word she said, Meghan Markle. I wouldn't believe it if she read me a weather report."

Morgan stormed off the programme after clashing with weather presenter Alex Beresford. His official departure from the show was later announced that evening. The following day, Morgan stood by his comments. He stated; "Freedom of speech is a hill I'm happy to die on."

Morgan later expressed that it was "not for me to question if she felt suicidal", but defended his "right to be allowed to have an opinion".

For his questioning of the validity of Meghan's claims about her mental health and suicidal thoughts, Morgan was criticised by mental health charity Mind.

Meghan and Harry's reasons for doing the interview with Oprah will always be known to them, and nobody else. Some will argue that the couple sought to clarify their position, and to explain the boundaries that they were seeking to have with the press. Others will insist that the interview was a last-ditch attempt to smear the reputations of those who the couple may have felt bitter towards. Ironically, if Meghan and Harry's reason for doing the interview was in order to get some peace and closure, it certainly caused a stir in the aftermath – particularly amongst the British media.

Regardless of why Meghan and Harry did the interview with Oprah, the very fact that *something* was a catalyst for their decision, cannot be ignored, and when looking at the British media's treatment of the couple, most would be hard-pressed to deny that there were certainly problems in the narrative that had been created about Meghan – prior to the interview, and prior to the couple's decision to step down as royals.

Chapter Six – The Yoko Effect

There are a great many parallels between Harry and Meghan, and John Lennon and Yoko Ono.

Let's start with John and Yoko. Yoko was given so much stick from many people who saw her as this god-awful woman who was solely responsible for the break-up of The Beatles. On balance, Yoko – both as an individual, and in her partnership with John Lennon – certainly had her fair share of fans. The fact is though, that when the media and the public wanted to spout their venomous opinions of her, there were plenty to go around.

The British tabloids were instrumental in pushing the narrative that Yoko was controlling and imposing – and frequently to the detriment of The Beatles' studio sessions, monopolising poor, innocent John. In 1970 (the year The Beatles officially parted ways), even *Good Housekeeping* magazine ran a feature titled "The women who broke up The Beatles" (in which they were also critical of Linda McCartney for the same reasons).

Whether or not Yoko was really a key catalyst for the break-up of The Beatles will probably remain as a historical, cultural and social debate that will never be answered. There were so many variables at play that nobody, no matter how passionate they may be about their opinion, will be able to say with certainty, whether or not Yoko was the band-destroying enemy that some have made her out to be.

The problem that a lot of people had with Yoko, was in how they saw her as the one woman who singlehandedly destroyed The Beatles. What's vital to consider here, is that at the time (and indeed, by many today), The Beatles were a massively big deal in popular culture. They were a band of so many firsts in terms of what they achieved, not just commercially, but in terms of how they wrote and performed their own songs, and in terms of how each band member was known by name, with their legions of fans screaming for them. For of course, many of the young women in Britain who had caught a serious case of Beatlemania had decided – partly from what they had read in their teen magazines, and partly from the joys of their own imaginations – what their favourite Beatle was like not just as an artist, but as a *person*.

In terms of the latter, not only were The Beatles about the music: they were a *brand* – and a heavily personified one. They had an identity. The media, and the fantasy it served to generate in the minds of The Beatles' fans, all fed into each other, full circle. As part of this, everyone – whether a passionate fan, or someone with more of a passing interest – had at least some kind of set idea as to what, and *who*, The Beatles were.

For many, when Yoko came along, it changed the perceptions that the public had come to know, and perhaps even love.

Whether or not Yoko "broke up The Beatles", she was plausibly a vital factor in terms of a change that happened in Lennon – even if she simply just brought out a side of him that had always been there.

"When Yoko came along, part of her attraction was her avant-garde side, her view of things," McCartney said in 2012. "So, she showed [Lennon] another way to be, which was very attractive to him."

In terms of his public persona, in his partnership with Yoko, John Lennon was, for many, no longer the same man they had come to know (well, "know", as it were). People's perceptions and ideas of John Lennon the man were changed when he was no longer "a Beatle", and all of a sudden, "with Yoko".

A lot of people were angered by this. There was a sense that Yoko had taken something away from them. As they saw it, she had destroyed their beloved band by luring Lennon away from the rest of the group; poor John was far too enchanted to be capable of questioning her (supposedly ulterior) motives. He was totally under her spell, and under her thumb. Now, whether or not that was truly the case, the fact is that many people saw it that way.

The same thing has happened for many years in the music industry, and in any number of different bands – so much so that there was a storyline dedicated to it in the mockumentary/rockumentary, *This Is Spinal Tap* (1984). The lead singer, David St. Hubbins, is completely on the ball, completely dedicated to his band, all until his girlfriend comes along, and, like a lost puppy, he follows her ideas (many of them awful) without question. It's the whole idea of the love-struck man who can no longer think for himself, who is under the spell of a domineering mistress, and who has blindly abandoned his true destiny (and fans).

So, back to Harry and Meghan, and there is certainly a similar theme. It would seem that a lot of the hate directed towards Meghan is on the basis that many people see her as this awful woman who took Harry away from who, and what, he was destined to be. Some people who are really passionate about a brand, a band, or an individual in the public eye, seem to grow into thinking that they have some kind of ownership, or at least, investment, in what that brand/band/person can or can't do – both personally and professionally.

Whilst no fan or casual observer has the right (or involvement in the first place) to try and dictate what someone in the public eye should choose to do with their life, it doesn't stop anyone from voicing their opinions, no matter how intense or volatile. This is exactly what has happened, at least to an extent, in the case of Harry and Meghan. Many in the media seem to have insinuated that prior to meeting Meghan, Harry was going to live the life of any other male heir to the thrown – keeping quiet, doing "what's right", and dutifully sticking to the plan.

But Harry didn't do that, and it is often assumed that Meghan is the reason for this, and so, as some perhaps see it, she becomes fair game for all kinds of horrible remarks and nastiness. Meghan is, no matter what she does, or what she says, in many people's minds, the Yoko.

Isn't it fascinating how, in terms of some gender narratives, society has, for hundreds of years, insisted that men are strong-willed, stubborn, and in control of their life and career. As soon as they enter into a serious and committed relationship though, they are painted as being weak-willed and pliable, under the overbearing influence of a manipulative, controlling woman. The woman is portrayed as being almost witch-like. It's awful. Is Meghan currently suffering the same treatment in terms of how some of the media portray her, and in terms of the narrative that some of the general public support? There is a valid argument that yes, she is.

Chapter Seven – Haven't We Been Here Before?

O f all of the other women who have married into the royal family, Meghan has been most abundantly compared to two of them – and for very different reasons. On the basis of how she has shaken things up and been a figure of controversy, she has been compared to Wallace Simpson, the twice-divorced American who married Edward VIII on 3rd June 1937. In terms of those who seek to negate the difficulties that Meghan speaks of, a comparison to Catherine Middleton is commonly drawn, with many arguing something along the lines of "Kate was able to fit in straight away. If she managed it, then why can't Meghan?" (and with that, comes the insinuation that it is Meghan, and nobody else, who has the problem).

I'll get back to the Wallace Simpson comparison further along in this chapter. It matters. First though, let's start with Kate Middleton. After all, both Kate and Meghan are of the same generation and indeed, subject to a similar type of media culture (that said, Meghan has previously alluded to the idea that when Kate's engagement to William was made public in 2010, social media was different; it wasn't prominent to the extent that it is today in terms of how people use it to group together to speak against an individual).

Even if we are to say that social media hasn't changed that much in the time between Kate becoming a royal versus Meghan becoming a royal, the fact is that the British media certainly feeds into the mindset that many people take with them when it comes to participating in online bullying, something that Meghan has complained of.

"But surely, Kate had the same challenges with the British newspapers that Meghan has had?!" some people might declare, in hopes of their rhetoric being proven correct. Err, well, no actually. She hasn't.

Just take a look at some of these gems from the UK tabloids. In many instances, they are reporting on exactly the same outcomes. When applied to Kate, the stories are told in a way that makes her sound sweet, endearing, and thoughtful. When Meghan does *exactly the same things*, they are presented with an entirely different narrative – one that suggests she is callous, selfish, and in some cases, just plain weird and deluded.

Regarding Kate's choice of flowers:

In August 2011, *The Daily Express* reported; "As far as bridal bouquets go there was nothing particularly regal about Kate Middleton's modest arrangement of simple, seasonal flowers. Like the bride herself the bouquet was effortlessly elegant and understated… Yet behind that modest posy lay a secret story. Kate, the commoner-turned-duchess, had painstakingly selected blooms with real meaning. She is evidently well-versed in the language of flowers, a little-known romantic relic from the 19th century… Hence the use of lilac in her bouquet, which signifies the first emotions of love, the lily of the valley meaning a return of happiness, hyacinth standing for constancy, myrtle meaning love and the ivy, which represents fidelity. Then of course there was the suitably named Sweet William, which is shorthand for gallantry."

Regarding Meghan's choice of flowers:

In October 2019, *The Daily Express* ran the headline, "Royal Wedding: How Meghan Markle's flowers may have put Princess Charlotte's life at risk." Even going so far as to include a photograph of Charlotte sneezing, the report said, "[Meghan Markle] was holding a wedding bouquet which flowers were replicated in Princess Charlotte and the other bridesmaids' flower crowns. Express.co.uk can now reveal the children' [sic] crowns were made of flowers that can be deadly, especially for children. Meghan's bouquet was made of forget-me-nots as well as sweet peas, lily of the valley, astilbe, jasmine, and astrantia... Lily of the valley is a highly poisonous woodland flowering plant and ingestion could be deadly... As Meghan's bridesmaids were so young, having this flower on their heads could be considered a dangerous decision."

Regarding Kate's choice of room scent:

From *The Daily Mail* in May 2011: "It was reported that new Duchess of Cambridge requested her favourite scented candles and toiletries from luxury fragrance brand Jo Malone be delivered to scent the Abbey. A selection of candles, handwashes and lotions was requested, specifically in citrus spring scents including Orange Blossom, Grapefruit and the ever-popular Lime, Basil & Mandarin."

Regarding Meghan's choice of room scent:

In November 2018, the same paper went with this

headline: "Kicking up a stink: 'Dictatorial' bride Meghan wanted air fresheners for 'musty' 15th-century St George's Chapel… but the Palace said no." The article said, "Meghan wanted staff to go around with these atomisers, like spritzer guns, and spray the chapel with scent before anyone arrived. Royal Household staff stepped in and told her office politely, but firmly, that this was the Queen's chapel and it simply wasn't appropriate."

Regarding Kate's baby bump:

In March 2018, *The Daily Mail*'s headline was "Not long to go! Pregnant Kate tenderly cradles her baby bump while wrapping up her royal duties ahead of maternity leave – and William confirms 'she's due any minute now'." The paper said, "Bumping along nicely! The Duchess was seen placing a protective hand on her tummy."

Regarding Meghan's baby bump:

In January 2019, the same publication ran with the headline, "Why can't Meghan Markle keep her hands off her bump? Experts tackle the question that has got the nation talking: Is it pride, vanity, acting – or a new age bonding technique?"

Liz Jones, a columnist for the paper, added; "Personally, I find the cradling a bit like those signs in the back of cars: Baby on Board. Virtue signalling, as though the rest of us barren harridans deserve to burn alive in our cars. I do wonder what is to come once Meghan begins to breastfeed… will she milk it for all she's worth?"

Jo Elvin, editor of *You* magazine, was quoted in the same feature; "Meghan's positioning is always so fixed into one singular, rigid pose that it's becoming uncomfortable to watch. I'm getting arm aches just looking. It's all very Baby Bump Barbie… It smacks to me of a focus that's contrived and relentlessly photo-op ready. Meghan would be well advised to take the 'world's only pregnant woman!' vibes down a notch or two."

Regarding Kate's morning sickness:

Said *The Daily Express* in September 2017, "Kate's morning sickness cure? Prince William gifted with an avocado for pregnant Duchess." The feature stated: "Prince William was given one of the green fruit – wrapped up in a bow – by a little boy who's [sic] mother is suffering during her pregnancy too."

Regarding Meghan's morning sickness:

From the same publication in January 2019: "Meghan Markle's beloved avocado linked to human rights abuse and drought, millennial shame." The feature stated, "The pregnant Duchess of Sussex and so-called 'avocado on toast whisperer' is wolfing down a fruit linked to water shortages, illegal deforestation and all round general environmental devastation."

In the same month, *The Daily Mail* ran with the headline, "How Meghan's favourite avocado snack – beloved of all millennials – is fuelling human rights abuses, drought and murder."

When the Queen couldn't make it to a Christening hosted by Kate and William:

The Daily Mail said in July 2018: "The Queen and the Duke of Edinburgh missed the small family affair. The decision is understood not to have been taken on health grounds, and to have been mutually agreed by the Queen and the Cambridges some time ago. The Queen, ninety-two, has a busy week ahead, with high-profile celebrations in central London marking the centenary of the RAF on Tuesday, and a visit by US President Donald Trump in Windsor on Friday."

When the Queen couldn't make it to a Christening hosted by Meghan and Harry:

The same paper said in July 2019: "The situation

has surprised some senior staff at Buckingham Palace, who feel that the Duke and Duchess should have planned the day better. 'There is huge support for the couple in not wanting to conform to tradition. They are young, they are striking out on a different path from other members of the royal family and there is enormous goodwill for them. But they shouldn't do that without regard for tradition,' said one. 'Her Majesty was already scheduled to be in Scotland for her annual Holyrood Week and had a prior engagement at the weekend. There is a feeling amongst some that they should have been more accommodating about the date'."

Regarding Kate's Christmas plans:

From *The Daily Mail* in December 2016: "Carole wins granny war! Duke and Duchess of Cambridge will spend second 'private' Christmas with the Middleton family rather than joining the Queen at Sandringham." The feature continued with, "Royal sources said yesterday that the Queen understood and endorsed William and Kate's decision not to spend Christmas Day with her. One said: 'Her Majesty understands that it is a dilemma that many young couples face and acknowledges how close Catherine's relationship is with her family'."

Regarding Meghan's Christmas plans:

The same paper said in November 2019; "Doesn't the Queen deserve better than this baffling festive absence? Richard Kay examines the impact of Prince Harry's and Meghan Markle's decision not to spend Christmas with the royal family." Kay wrote; "The fact is the Queen expects to have the family around her for the festive season... to the Queen, for whom the tradition of the family gathering is a key date in her calendar, Harry and Meghan's absence will be a matter of great sadness. It will also be a source of frustration."

Regarding Kate's participation in a business project:

From *The Daily Mail* in January 2014: "Kate and Wills Inc: Duke and Duchess secretly set up companies to protect their brand – just like the Beckhams." Rebecca English wrote; "Creating their own companies will allow William and Kate to bring out, should they ever choose to, myriad items of officially-endorsed merchandise from tea towels to coffee cups... Kensington Palace officials said they were doing the 'sensible thing' in protecting the couple's rights."

Regarding Meghan's participation in a business project:

From the same publication in January 2020; "A

right royal cash in! How Prince Harry and Meghan Markle trademarked over 100 items from hoodies to socks in SIX MONTHS before split with monarchy – with new empire worth up to £400m." The paper added; "The Sussexes want to stamp their name on dozens of products including t-shirts, hoodies, journals and gloves for their newly-created foundation Sussex Royal... Experts said Harry and Meghan were actively preparing to quit the royal family months ago by filing trademark applications to commercially protect their brand."

Regarding Kate and William's approach to the loss of Princess Diana:

A headline from *The Sun* in April 2017: "STIFF UPPER FLIP. Prince William blasts monarchy's 'stiff upper lip' tradition and backs Harry's admission of his mental anguish after death of mother Diana." The feature continued, "Prince William yesterday backed brother Harry's brave admission of his mental anguish – and blasted the monarchy's 'stiff upper lip' tradition... William said: 'There may be a time and a place for the 'stiff upper lip' but not at the expense of your health... Catherine and I are clear we want both George and Charlotte to grow up feeling able to talk about their emotions and feelings'."

Regarding Meghan and Harry's approach to the

loss of Princess Diana:

In October 2019, the same publication ran the headline, "ROYAL RIFTS. Prince Harry and Meghan ditched British stiff upper lip – is this a good thing? *Sun* parents and kids are torn." The feature stated; "What you make of 'fragile' Prince Harry and Meghan's comments may depend on your generation. *Sun* parents and kids reveal what they think of the Duke and Duchess of Sussex airing their emotions in public – and whether they have the right to moan in such positions of privilege."

Take note of how, in the last example there, Harry wasn't given a hard time when mentioned in his capacity as William's brother. Overall, the above shows that no matter what Meghan does or doesn't do, when it comes to the British media, she can't win. If the same events were given a positive spin when Kate engaged in them, then there is absolutely no reason as to why the same couldn't have been done for Meghan. It is evident that there is a pattern here, and that to compare Meghan's journey to Kate's is unfair in the sense that Kate hasn't been given a hard time in the same way that Meghan has.

Now, back to Wallace Simpson. The circumstances surrounding her difficulties in being romantically involved with a royal were very different, not just on the basis that it was a different time, with different people, but on the basis of the way that the British media worked back then.

Wallace Simpson didn't have to undergo trial by British newspaper in the way that Meghan (or, to be fair, Kate) has. Simpson's involvement with Edward VIII was only made public knowledge through the UK media at the very last hour, as it were.

A lot of the difficulties that Edward VIII and Wallace faced were in relation to what went on behind the scenes, rather than them being thrust into the limelight by the media. Edward's parents (George V and Mary) refused to formally meet Wallace, and ultimately, would not go on to attend the wedding.

In the UK, throughout the majority of Edward's tenure as King, all mention of Wallace was very much censored. The average citizen outside of the inner society of royalty would have been blissfully unaware of the controversial relationship.

The US press had already been positive towards Wallace, painting her as an American success story in her association with Edward. In Britain, such was the power that royalty had over the press that it was possible to keep the public in the dark about anything that was deemed too troublesome to bring to light. Edward and Wallace's relationship had been going on for at least a full year before the British papers finally told the public anything about it. Prior to that, all media from abroad was intercepted at ports, the information cut out and destroyed by distributors who didn't want to be held responsible for the outbreak of a scandal. When any politician spoke to lobby correspondents of Edward and Wallace's relationship, the British press didn't report on it.

As owner of *The Daily Express* at the time, Lord Beaverbrook fully supported the King's request "to protect Wallis from sensational publicity at least in my own country". Beaverbrook managed to persuade other publications to take the same approach.

When editor of *The Times*, Geoffrey Dawson, paid a visit with C.P. Scott of *The Manchester Guardian* to Downing Street, they found out that Prime Minister Stanley Baldwin felt strongly that the public would find a relationship between their King and an American divorcee offensive. It soon became clear to them that there was little to be gained from breaking the requested confidence.

It was easy for the majority of the British press to

be wholly supportive of what the establishment was asking for in terms of confidentiality. Nobody wanted to open a can of worms that could divide public opinion and compromise British confidence in the monarchy.

Finally, the secret could no longer be contained. On 16th November 1936, Edward invited Stanley Baldwin to Buckingham Palace, where he explained that once Wallace's divorce from Ernest Aldrich Simpson had been finalised, he planned to marry her. Baldwin warned the King that the public would deem such a marriage to be morally unacceptable; not only was marriage post-divorce opposed by the Church of England, but the people would not accept Simpson as Queen. As King, Edward was the titular head of the church, and there was an expectation on him to stand in union with the institutional teachings. The Archbishop of Canterbury, Cosmo Gordon Lang, was adamant that Edward must stand down as King, as was the British Cabinet, who rejected Edward's suggestion of a morganatic marriage whereby Wallace Simpson would not become Queen.

With the monarchy at crisis point, from 3rd December onwards, most papers were relatively kind in their initial reporting of Edward and Wallace's relationship. Even the more disparaging of headlines came across as being on the fence, rather than as outright accusatory. On 5th December, *The Mirror* demanded, "The nation insists on knowing the king's full demands and conditions. The country will give you a verdict."

Edward and Wallace, in a way, didn't have to face the music when it came to what *The Mirror*, or indeed, the public, may have wanted. On 11th December 1936, less than a week after his involvement with Wallace had first been announced in the British press, Edward's abdication of the throne was made public. On 12th December, his younger brother, the Duke of York, was proclaimed King George VI.

A small affair with a relatively small number of guests, the wedding of Edward VIII and Wallace Simpson took place at the Château de Candé in France, on 3rd June 1937.

Now then, just like Wallace, Meghan came to the royal family as a divorcee, and an American one at that! Neither woman represents the package of what was/is expected and desired for a King/heir to the throne to be married to. However, when it comes to comparing Wallace Simpson's experience (or lack thereof) of the British media with Meghan's, that's arguably where the similarities end. It would be unfair to say that Wallace had it easy (she quickly left Britain and fled to France as the scandal broke, desperately trying to outrun the then-engaged press by that point), but certainly, less than a week of awkwardness with the more humble British papers of the day, is worlds away from the years that Meghan has endured.

It's not just the fact that Meghan's scrutiny under the British media has been longer in duration, it's that it has been more brutal and disparaging too. Whereas the British press back in Wallace's day was willing to keep quiet when asked, and be respectful when finally reporting, the version of the British press that Meghan has had to deal with have a different approach entirely. They have a strong tendency to be hungry and ruthless, with little concern for the impact that their reporting could have on not only the monarchy, but on individuals within it. In a world that has changed exponentially since the days of Edward and Wallace's relationship, scandal not only sells, but when it comes to the British media, is an outright currency.

In December 2022, Anna Pasternak, author of *The American Duchess: The Real Wallis Simpson*, wrote for *The Telegraph* that Meghan and Wallace's experiences aren't alike – in the sense that whilst Meghan has gone public with her displeasure at the royal institution, and has apparently burned many bridges in the process, Wallace worked hard to heal the rift between

Edward and his mother. Unbeknownst to Edward, Wallace penned a letter to Mary where she apologised for "any separation that exists between Mother and Son".

Pasternak's point is an interesting one; it highlights how Wallace apparently didn't wish for there to be any animosity within the royal family as a result of her involvement with Edward. Would it be fair or appropriate, though, to suggest that Meghan wants an all-out drama, and severing of personal ties, when it comes to Harry's relationship with his birth family? When looking at the way in which Meghan seems to have made the effort to engage with the royal family initially – especially in the build-up towards, and straight after her marriage to Harry – it would seem reasonable to assume that this hasn't been the case.

Chapter Eight – Sparkle like Markle

I first encountered the phrase 'Sparkle like Markle' when I read it on a t-shirt in Primark. There were loads of them, in an array of sweet pastel and bold colours, displayed in various arrangements on the shop floor, their ironed-on metallic slogans reflecting in the spotlights as you go up the escalator to the underwear floor.

At the time, when I saw those t-shirts, I thought the concept was, dare I say it, a bit sycophantic. As someone who wasn't (and still isn't) a royalist, I thought it was a bit much to invest in a t-shirt that would hold relevance for all of one week. Not only that, but I found the hype a bit bizarre at the time. Your mileage may vary. That's cool.

Now though, I wouldn't mind having one of those t-shirts – not, however, in relation to how, at the time, Ms Markle was due to marry into royalty and become a princess. It's not about the fairytale anymore. Meghan Markle, and what she represents, runs far deeper than who she is as the woman who got married to Prince Harry. She is so much more than that. I passionately hope that overall, in the long run, the mainstream British media – and indeed, those who consume it – will not only see that, but celebrate it too. I mean, if every single person in the world were to do just a fraction of the charity work, activism and advocacy that Meghan has done, then wow, what a world it would be. If someone were to advise anyone to Sparkle like Markle, it would surely be one hell of a compliment.

This book has been written at what is probably the peak of a challenging time for Meghan Markle. Later down the line, it may just serve to stand as a snapshot in time. The media being the fickle vehicle that it is (particularly the British press), it is entirely possible that their overall narrative on her could change once again, to something that is more positive and less disparaging. We'll just have to watch this space.

Chapter Eight

www.ingramcontent.com/pod-product-compliance
Lightning Source LLC
Chambersburg PA
CBHW052130030426
42337CB00028B/5103

* 9 7 8 1 9 1 3 7 7 9 9 0 0 *